PRO
CHICAG
CHRISTIAN SCHOOL

P9-BYJ-497

WHEN CHICAGO WAS YOUNG

in 1835, it was a rough and tumble frontier town. Log cabins and clapboard houses rose haphazardly beside muddy roads. Sailing ships were anchored far offshore. By night, pioneer campfires lit the skies. By day, the streets teemed with children laughing; pigs, chickens, and cows roamed about; blue-coated army officers mingled with Indians, peddlers, and busy settlers eager to start a new life.

These were the rude beginnings of a city whose factories and waterways would soon make her "Queen of the West"—a city whose past bore such glamorous names as Marquette and Jolliet, her discoverers, and Point du Sable, the mysterious and romantic black man who was the real founder of Chicago. From her founding, through boom times, to the disastrous Great Chicago Fire, exciting accounts of people who actually were there bring the smell of stockyards and smoke and the sound of chugging railroad engines right to the written page. Old prints, engravings, and color illustrations illuminate the lively text.

This book is one of the *How They Lived* series, developed by Garrard to give meaning to the study of American history. Young people will find a deeper understanding and more lasting appreciation of history and geography as they see life in the past through the eyes of those who lived it.

PROPERTY OF
CHICAGO SOUTHWEST
CHRISTIAN SCHOOL

Courtesy Chicago Historical Society

When Chicago Was Young

When Chicago Was Young

BY JAMES McCAGUE

ILLUSTRATED BY RAYMOND BURNS

GARRARD PUBLISHING COMPANY
CHAMPAIGN, ILLINOIS

Picture credits:

Chicago Historical Society: p. 1, 5, 8, 16 (bottom), 19, 26, 28, 32, 41, 47, 72

Culver Pictures: p. 63, 76, back cover

Historical Pictures Service, Chicago: p. 13, 15, 16 (top), 21, 54, 85, 86-87, 90

Kogan, Herman and Lloyd Wendt, *Chicago: A Pictorial History*,
   (New York: E. P. Dutton and Company, Inc., 1958): p. 24, 50

Library of Congress: p. 48, 56 (bottom), 68, 70, 78, 83

Memorial Hall Library, Andover, Massachusetts: p. 56 (top)

Picture Collection, New York Public Library: p. 89

Endsheets: *Chicago in 1857,* a lithograph after the drawing by James T. Palmatary.
   Courtesy of Chicago Historical Society.

Copyright © 1971 by James McCague
All rights reserved. Manufactured in the U.S.A.
Standard Book Number: 8116-6925-4
Library of Congress Catalog Card Number: 77-126414

Courtesy Chicago Historical Society

Contents

1. Potawatomi Farewell

One sunny August day in the year 1835, a stir of excitement ran through the little frontier town of Chicago. People looked at one another, frowning. They had not expected any Indian trouble, but now—who knew what might happen?

Shrill war whoops filled the air. Indian drums made of sections of hollow logs with skin stretched over the ends boomed loudly. Warriors pranced about. They wore nothing but breech-clouts: strips of hide or bark cloth twisted around their hips. They had painted their bodies and faces with stripes of red and yellow and blue war paint and they all had weapons. Some fired muskets into the air.

Courtesy Chicago Historical Society

Simple wooden buildings lined the riverbank of
the new village. Its first public school is at left.

Indian women in buckskin dresses clapped and
shouted. Indian boys and girls ran about, playing
and shouting too. These people belonged to the
powerful Potawatomi tribe. Five thousand of them
were camped around Chicago.

The town itself wasn't very big. Most of its
buildings were cabins made of logs or wooden slabs
called clapboards that had been split from tree
trunks with an ax. Only a few thousand settlers
lived there, and on this day they all stayed close
to their homes. No doubt many were badly
frightened—and no wonder.

Most of this land in the northern part of
Illinois had once belonged to the Potawatomis.

Some time before, however, the chiefs had held a council and agreed to sell it to the white men. In return they were promised barrels of whiskey, bales of blankets and other trade goods, and a sum of money. They were also promised new lands in the west, far across the Mississippi River.

Many white men knew, though, that they had cheated the Potawatomis. Now they thought the red men might be angry and refuse to keep their bargain.

Peering from their windows, they saw the Indians swarming into town.

First came the medicine men, thumping on the drums and shaking rattles made of hollow gourds filled with pebbles. Eight hundred warriors followed, leaping high in the air and brandishing their weapons. Squaws and children scurried along behind. The thudding drums, the rattles, the screaming from thousands of throats, all made a frightful noise. On came the Indians, streaming through the dusty dirt streets.

At each house they stopped and went into a war dance. The warriors lashed out violently with tomahawks and war clubs, as if they were killing make-believe enemies. Whipping out their knives, they bent down and went through the motions of scalping fallen foes. Their eyes gleamed. Sweat ran down their bodies, smearing the war paint into weird patterns.

Stories written by people who were in Chicago

that day tell us that many women in the houses hid their faces, afraid to watch. Some of them fainted. Small boys and girls cried and clung to their mothers' skirts. Nervous men barred the doors, wondering what would happen next.

A man named John Caton had come to town just a short while before. Many years afterward he would become chief justice of the state of Illinois. He told how he looked out from the inn where he was staying. All he could think of was that the Indians seemed like demons—evil spirits from another world.

"How easy it would have been for them to massacre us all!" he wrote.

In the end, however, the Indians all went on to the gate of Fort Dearborn. The fort, a big log building, stood near the place where the Chicago River flowed into Lake Michigan. Officers of the United States Army were waiting there. They handed over the money and trade goods promised.

Still shouting and prancing, the Potawatomis made their way back to their camp outside the town. All day long, and far into the night, campfires blazed and war whoops rang out among the

wigwams. Then at last the Indians fell asleep, worn out by the show they had put on.

Next morning they began to pack up their belongings. Within a few days, they loaded them onto packhorses and set out for the west. The wild war dances, the shouting, the make-believe battles—all these had been merely their way of saying good-bye forever to their old homeland.

In fact, it was a rather pitiful thing, for the Potawatomis were a proud, brave people. But they knew they could no longer hold out against the hordes of white settlers and their new, strange ways.

As for Chicago, it still had a long way to go before it would be much of a town. It was growing fast, though. Its people were hard workers. They had made up their minds to stay, and many of them already had come through some hard and bitter times.

2. The Crossing Place

Long before any white men went there, the Indians used the spot called Checagou as a portage, or crossing place.

No one is sure what their word *checagou* really means. Some people claim it is an Indian name for the wild garlic weeds that grew along the bank of the muddy river that flows into Lake Michigan at that point. Others think there once was a wise old chief by that name. Still others believe it comes from a similar Indian word, meaning *skunk*.

At any rate, the Indians found that they could paddle their canoes up the river from the lake, and then carry them across a short stretch of land to another river, the Des Plaines, which flows to the southwest. The Des Plaines presently joins still another river, the Illinois. And the Illinois, in its turn, empties into the mighty Mississippi.

Thus, this crossing place offered them a good way to move from the northeastern regions of America to the lands far to the south and west.

Very few Indians ever made such a long, wearisome journey. But hunting parties often traveled part of the way, for the plains beside the Illinois River teemed with buffalo, deer, and other wild game. The various tribes traded with each other, also. They exchanged things like animal pelts, pottery, axes and arrowheads made of flint, and so on. Many of these Indian goods were carried back and forth across the portage.

No tribe cared to live there, though. The land was low and swampy. In rainy weather much of it was covered with mud. The lakeshore was only barren sand, heaped by winds and waves into low hills, called sand dunes. So Checagou remained a crossing place, and nothing more.

Then, one fall day in the long-ago year of 1673, several white men and Indian guides paddled birchbark canoes up the Des Plaines River. They made camp near the lake. Their leader, a sturdy, keen-eyed young man in buckskin clothing, looked about him.

He was interested in everything he saw, for

Marquette and Jolliet are greeted near Checagou
by friendly Indians bearing peace pipes.

he had come to explore this land. He was a
Frenchman named Louis Jolliet.

Among his companions was a gentle, gray-haired
man who wore a long black robe. A silver
crucifix hung on a chain around his neck. This
man was a priest, Father Jacques Marquette.
He had come to America to preach the Christian
religion to the Indians.

As far as we know, these were the first white
men to visit Checagou. They soon headed north,
for their home base was in New France, or
present-day Canada. But Louis Jolliet had seen
at once how the crossing place could help France
to build a great empire in America.

Pioneer black trader Point du Sable, left, lived in this cabin near the Chicago River. When he left, his cabin became the home of John Kinzie.

Courtesy Chicago Historical Society

In his report to the governor of New France, he suggested that a canal be dug across the portage. Then, he wrote, Frenchmen could travel in ships or canoes all the way from New France to the Gulf of Mexico. Traders, soldiers, and settlers would find the journey easier, and much faster, than trying to struggle through the dense forests on land.

It was a wonderful dream, but Jolliet never saw it come true. Nearly 200 years would pass before that happened.

In the meantime, France and England fought a great war. England finally won all of New France and most of the land east of the Mississippi River. Then, a few years later, some of the English settlers in America rebelled against their mother country. A new nation, the United States of America, was born.

During those long, troubled years, a grubby little village slowly grew up at the crossing place. Sometimes its name was spelled Chickago, and sometimes Chicago. It consisted of nothing but a few huts and Indian wigwams. No one thought it had much of a future until Jean Baptiste Point du Sable moved there in 1782. He, more than anyone else, was the real founder of Chicago.

Point du Sable married a Potawatomi woman named Catherine. He began to trade for furs with the Indians of the region. He was a black man, and apparently quite a mysterious, romantic figure, for no one knew him very well. He told many different stories about himself.

At times, he said he came from an island far off in the West Indies. Then again, he claimed to be a Potawatomi chief. Some people thought he had once been a slave, but had run away from his master. At any rate, he was a good trader. He got along with the Indians, and his business prospered. He built a big log house and filled it with fine furniture and costly paintings hauled in wagons all the way from eastern cities.

Encouraged by his success, other men brought their families and built cabins nearby.

Then, quite suddenly, Point du Sable sold all his property to another trader and went away. To this day, nobody knows why. It seemed a strange thing to do, just when things were going so well. Before long it seemed stranger still, for the other settlers heard some good news.

A troop of soldiers marched into the village one day. The United States government wanted a new fort on the Lake Michigan shore, and Chicago had been chosen as the site.

The soldiers took almost a year to build Fort Dearborn, as it was called. But when it was finished, they had done their work well. The fort was enclosed by a stout stockade of logs, twelve feet high. Two large blockhouses armed with cannons stood at opposite corners. Inside were large rooms where the officers and soldiers ate and slept, and a big stone building where gunpowder was stored.

Life around the fort became quite pleasant. Traders lived in snug cabins on the riverbanks. Settlers drove their cattle in from nearby farms and sold them for beef to feed the soldiers. Now and then, small sailing ships dropped anchor offshore. They brought supplies and trade goods, and took on cargoes of furs and smoked meat.

When they were off duty, the soldiers fished or swam or went hunting. Sometimes they put

The first Fort Dearborn in the village of Chicago

Courtesy Chicago Historical Society

on field days, with footraces and wrestling matches. Friendly Indians often joined in. Once in a while a trader named John Kinzie brought his fiddle to the fort. Then settlers and soldiers and their wives would have a dance.

Unfortunately, these good times didn't last long. In the year 1812, war broke out between the United States and England.

It came about because the captains of English warships insisted on stopping and searching American ships at sea. They sometimes forced American sailors to join English crews. All this was far away from Chicago, of course. It meant very little to the folk there.

But suddenly, and terribly, the war struck home to them.

3. Fort Dearborn Falls

Captain Nathan Heald, the commander at Fort Dearborn, was a worried man. A messenger had just brought him a letter from the general in charge of all the American troops in the region. It contained bad news.

Englishmen were giving guns to some Indian tribes nearby. They were saying that the English army would drive the Americans away. Then all the land would be given back to the Indians, they promised, in return for their help in the war. Many of the tribes believed this. They were going on the warpath.

Captain Heald had only 55 soldiers: not enough to put up a good defense. Therefore, the letter

ordered him to leave Fort Dearborn and march
to some stronger, safer place farther east.

Calling his officers together, he told them of
the order. As they talked it over, a friendly
Potawatomi chief named Black Partridge came to
the fort. He too had bad news.

"We can no longer be friends," said the chief
sadly.

Some of his young warriors were eager to
attack the fort, he explained. He couldn't hold
them off much longer.

The captain offered him a bargain. If the
Potawatomis would let the Americans go in peace,

he would leave most of the food and other supplies in the fort for them. Black Partridge agreed.
But there was no time to lose, he warned. Two
other tribes, the Winnebagos and the Kickapoos,
were also ready to attack.

On a sultry morning in August, the soldiers
marched out of Fort Dearborn. Tramping through
the sand, they headed south along the lakeshore.
Most of the traders and settlers around Chicago
were with them. The women and children rode
in two wagons at the rear of the column, followed by twelve militiamen. Some of the women
had tiny babies in their arms.

23

The little band had gone about a mile and a half when the soldiers saw warriors in war paint sticking their heads up from the sand dunes where they were hiding. Captain Heald at once ordered his men to charge and drive them away.

Stumbling forward through the sand, they were met by a blast of gunfire. Some of the soldiers fell. Yelling warriors swarmed out from behind the dunes and surrounded the rest. Other Indians made straight for the two wagons. Grimly the Americans fought back. Even the women fought, snatching up knives, axes, anything else at hand.

Mrs. Heald bravely battles the warriors in an Indian attack on the wagon train.

But they were no match for the horde of blood-thirsty warriors. In ten minutes, it was all over.

Black Partridge, and other friendly chiefs, managed to save a few traders and their families. Captain Heald led some of his men to the top of a sand dune. From there, again and again, they fought off their attackers. At last the enemy warriors offered to spare their lives if the captain would promise to have the United States government pay a ransom of $100 for each soldier. Then Nathan Heald surrendered. His men threw down their weapons and were taken prisoner.

Out of 95 people who started from the fort, however, only 43 were left alive.

That night the victorious warriors howled in glee as they burned Fort Dearborn to the ground.

Courtesy Chicago Historical Society

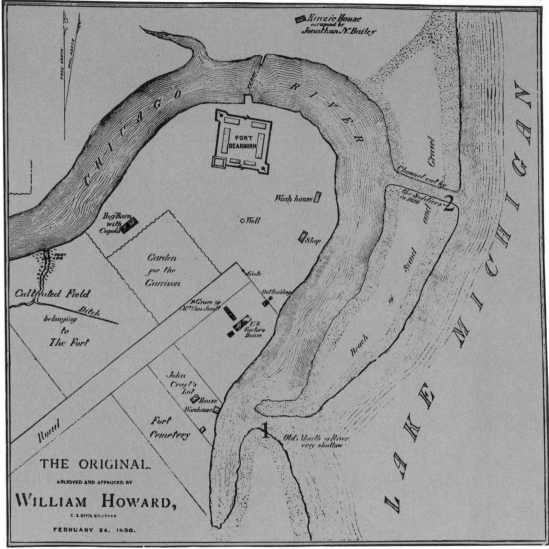

This map shows Chicago as it looked in 1830. Because the mouth of the river (1) was shallow, a channel to Lake Michigan (2) had been cut in 1828. Now ships of all kinds could sail into the Chicago River.

4. "You're in It, Stranger!"

Fort Dearborn's destruction didn't mean that the war was over. American forces rallied. After long, hard fighting, they finally beat the English and their Indian allies. Peace came again.

After some years, American soldiers returned to the old crossing place. They built a new Fort Dearborn on the ruins of the old one. The bones of the massacre victims were buried. Once more, settlers began to move west. A new village grew up around the fort. For a long time, though, visitors to the place weren't very much impressed with it. One man, who went there in 1830, even

27

had a hard time finding it. Said he, in a letter to a friend:

"I hit the woods to the northeast. Then I wandered down upon a half-dozen log houses and asked about Chicago. 'You're in it, stranger,' they told me."

That was scarcely an exaggeration. The village straggled helter-skelter along both banks of the Chicago River. Pigs, chickens, and cows roamed wherever they pleased. Settlers often had to seize their guns, call their dogs, and go out to chase away wolves or bears that prowled nearby.

Without fear of Indian attacks, children could play safely inside the new Fort Dearborn.

Courtesy Chicago Historical Society

Nevertheless, some men had faith in Chicago's future. In that same year of 1830, they hired a surveyor to lay out a town of 48 square blocks. True, most of those blocks existed only on the map. In wet weather, many of them still lay deep under mud or water. It didn't matter; Chicago could call itself a town at last.

It had fewer than 40 buildings, and no more than 200 people lived there.

Yet the town had an air of busy, bustling life about it. Soon it began to grow more rapidly. Many folk came to make farms for themselves on the good prairie lands to the north and west. Many others hoped to start businesses, or find work, or just have a look at the wild, rough frontier.

Some came trudging through the mud and sand along Lake Michigan's southern shore. Their children and household goods were piled in wagons hauled by horses or oxen. Often, at night, dozens of their campfires glowed and flickered in the open country all around the town.

Some came down through the Great Lakes in sailing schooners. It was a hard, uncomfortable voyage, for the ships were small and cramped. A young man from Vermont named James Cobb has left us a record of his trip. He had to sleep on the deck with no shelter but a blanket. Rain frequently drenched him. Sometimes it stormed, and waves swept over him.

29

When they arrived at Chicago, the schooner had to anchor far offshore, for there was no harbor. A huge sandbar blocked the mouth of the Chicago River, so the passengers went ashore in canoes or rowboats.

Poor James Cobb, however, was kept on board for three long days. He had paid a fare of four dollars: every cent he had in the world. But now the captain demanded three dollars more. Another passenger finally loaned young Cobb the money, so he could pay off the cheating captain. Then he was allowed to land.

Not everyone had such a rude welcome to Chicago, of course. But many were disgusted by what they found in the town. An English traveler by the name of Charles Latrobe, for example, wrote of seeing "sharpers of every degree; peddlers, grog-sellers, horse dealers and horse stealers...rogues of every description: white, black, brown and red..."

Latrobe went on to tell how "the little village was in an uproar from morning till night, and from night till morning...betting and gambling were the order of the day." He also complained that the inn where he stayed "was in a state of confusion, filth and racket."

No, indeed, Mr. Latrobe didn't like Chicago at all!

Because of so many travelers, the town had several inns. Nowadays, people would turn up

their noses at even the Sauganash Tavern, though it was the best of the lot. It was a big log building south of the river. Surly Indians wandered in and out, often full of rum or whiskey. The place was plagued by rats and mice. Jokers claimed there were only two blankets in the whole tavern. The minute a guest fell asleep, they said, his blanket was taken away and given to someone else.

But Mark Beaubien, the owner, was such a friendly, jolly host that folks quickly forgave him for his tavern's faults. He always wore a blue coat with shiny brass buttons, and liked to play the fiddle and sing songs to his guests in a big,

Indians, settlers, and livestock mingled casually in front of the first jail at Public Square in 1836.

Courtesy Chicago Historical Society

booming voice. Because of him, the Sauganash Tavern came to be known for miles around.

At times so many people crowded in that some had to sleep on the floor, or in the attic. Perhaps "Long John" Wentworth has left us a truer picture of those newcomers to Chicago than the sour Mr. Latrobe.

Long John was a young fellow who walked into town in the early 1830's. His nickname came from the fact that he was a lanky six feet, six inches tall. Many years later, after he had grown wealthy, and served as one of Chicago's most famous mayors, he wrote about the men and women he knew in those early days:

> We had people from almost every clime, and almost every opinion. We had Jews and Christians, Protestants, Catholics and infidels....Nearly every language was represented. Some people had seen much of the world, and some very little. Some were quite learned and some were ignorant....

Different though they were, most of these people had a few things in common. They were eager to get along, to make money, to find new and better homes for themselves here in the northwest. So many of them came, finally, that they forced the Potawatomis to sell their land and move away, as we have seen.

The new people brought some good things to Chicago.

Before long, boys and girls had a school to attend. It was just a room in an old stable, but it was a beginning. Soon there were several churches, too. A young printer brought his printing press from New York and started a newspaper called the *Chicago Democrat*. The town council passed a law providing a two-dollar fine for anyone who "let any hog run loose without a ring in its nose or a yoke around its neck."

The rough little town beside Lake Michigan was growing up.

5. Boom and Bust

Early in the morning on July 4, 1836, a big crowd of people gathered at the wooden bridge over the Chicago River. Everyone was laughing and talking happily. For them, this was more than just another Independence Day. They had a very special reason for wanting to celebrate.

Louis Jolliet's long-ago dream of a canal across the old Indian portage was going to come true at last.

Like Jolliet, many far-sighted men had realized for a long time that an all-water route from the Great Lakes to the Gulf of Mexico would be good for business and commerce. It would help not only Chicago, but the whole state of Illinois as well.

Indeed, the people of every nearby state would benefit too. Finally, the government and the public had been convinced of this.

Money had been raised by the sale of land along the route the canal would follow. Loans made by the state of Illinois provided additional funds. William Ogden, a leading Chicago businessman, had been given a contract to dig its eastern section. He had brought in a crew of brawny Irish workmen from the east. On this fine, bright Fourth of July, all was ready for the start.

BOOM! A cannon at Fort Dearborn fired a salute.

It went on firing, 52 times in all, as the people pushed their way on board three small ships moored near the bridge. One was a steamboat named the *Chicago*. The other two were sailing schooners: the *Llewellyn* and the *Sea Serpent*. Flags fluttered from their masts. Everyone cheered lustily as the ships cast off and started up the river.

The crowd was so large that not everybody could find room on the ships. Some folk climbed into wagons or carriages and followed along on the riverbank. Ladies in their best dresses and bonnets waved handkerchiefs. Boys and girls laughed and chattered in excitement. Many of the gentlemen rode horses.

Nearly every family had a picnic basket filled with good things to eat. Poor folk who had no

horses or wagons trudged along on foot. Nobody wanted to miss the fun.

Slowly the ships moved up the river a few miles, to a place called Canalport. That would be the eastern end of the canal. Everybody went ashore. Those who had followed on the riverbank came hurrying up. The crowd clapped and cheered as several men made patriotic speeches. They cheered more loudly still when a prominent citizen of Chicago named Simon Archer dug up the first shovelful of earth.

Now the Illinois and Michigan Canal, as it would be called, was under way. The picnic began.

By this time, some of the men were in a rollicking mood. Bringing up several boxes of lemons, they threw them into a little spring close by.

"There's lemonade for all you people who don't like hard liquor!" they shouted.

Then other men rolled up a barrel of whiskey. Gleefully, they poured the whiskey into the spring too. "Now the rest of us can have some punch!" one of them cried.

At length the long holiday was over. People started homeward, tired but happy. Then, as the *Chicago* steamed down the river, a gang of rough fellows appeared on the bank. They began to throw rocks at the people on board. Perhaps they had drunk a little too much of the "punch" from the spring. The men on the steamboat knew just what to do, though.

Quickly steering her to the bank again, they jumped ashore. There was a wild scuffle. Noses were bloodied and eyes were blackened. But six of the troublemakers were captured and locked in jail. So the day ended happily, after all.

The work on the canal brought boom times to Chicago. *Boom times* was an expression that meant business was very good. Jobs were plentiful. More and more people poured into the town. Most of them wanted to buy land, because they were sure it would soon increase in value. A tall Negro man in a red suit walked through the streets, calling out news about the land sales that were held each day. At every corner crowds thronged around him, eager to buy.

New businesses sprang up, and old ones were making more money than ever before. Along the Chicago River stood cattle pens and slaughterhouses, busy factories, lumberyards, and tanneries where leather was made.

There were some bad effects from all this growth, however. So much garbage and waste was

Courtesy Chicago Historical Society

A street vender hauls a barrelful of water through
the bustling streets of young Chicago in 1843.

dumped into the river that the water flowing into
Lake Michigan became foul and stinking. It was
scarcely fit to drink, or even to wash in.

Many rich folk preferred to buy water from
street venders, who filled barrels from lakes or
streams outside the town and hauled them in on
wagons. The price was ten cents a barrel.

Some of those rich folk were building fine
homes, too, but poor people often had to live in
wretched shacks built on stilts, to keep them out
of the mud. That mud still was one of Chicago's
worst handicaps. A few streets were paved with

wooden planks but, in most other streets, wagons and carts often got stuck so badly their drivers had to abandon them. Sometimes they remained stuck for days at a time.

The truth was that Chicago was growing *too* fast, but few people seemed to care. They kept right on buying land, often going into debt in order to do it. Some, impatient to sell again at a big profit, no longer wanted to work.

Then, suddenly, the boom times ended.

Banks began to fail, because they had loaned too much money to people who couldn't pay it back. Before long other businesses were going broke, too. Many of their owners lost every cent they had. Work on the Illinois and Michigan Canal stopped. There was no more money to pay the workmen.

Money became so scarce, in fact, that merchants had to do business with scrip. They printed slips of paper that read: GOOD FOR FIFTY CENTS AT OUR STORE, or GOOD FOR A SUIT OF CLOTHES, or GOOD FOR A SHAVE OR A HAIRCUT, and so on. Workingmen, and other merchants with goods to sell, had to accept scrip instead of money.

Chicago folk still were hardy pioneers, though. They had not really forgotten how to work. Grimly they went to work now, to pull themselves and their city out of the hard times.

Chicago had received a bad setback, but it was far from being beaten.

6. Queen of the Lakes

James Lawrence sat in his room in a boarding-house on Monroe Street, writing a letter to his wife, Sarah. He had recently come to Chicago from New York state to look for a new job. Evidently he liked Chicago, for he wrote:

> Here is the place where a man can be free. In a year or two, I will save enough for a farm. Our children can get a good education for nothing....

James Lawrence wasn't an important person at all. But because Sarah saved his letters, we know a great deal of what a plain workingman thought about the bustling city on Lake Michigan. In

another letter he told of his job in a new factory that was being built.

He worked pretty long hours. "I leave at four o'clock in the morning and get home at six in the afternoon," he wrote. Then he went on to say that his wages were $1.50 a day. He thought it was very good pay. It seems that Sarah had some doubts about Chicago, for he added: "You would like it here. If you would take one look at these beautiful prairies, all your sadness would flee...."

After a while Lawrence got a better job that paid $15.00 a week. Happily he wrote to Sarah that he was sending her the money for steamboat fare. That's about all we really know of the Lawrences, though we may assume that she did finally join her husband in Chicago. What she thought when she arrived, we can only imagine.

It was 1858 now. Good times had followed bad, bringing vast growth and many changes to the city. It was dirtier, noisier, more crowded than ever but it was busier and more prosperous, too. Surely Sarah and her children must have been amazed as their steamboat chugged slowly up the Chicago River to its dock.

The river was literally choked with other steamboats, sailing ships and barges. Sailors swaggered in and out of taverns on the riverbanks. Bosses shouted orders to sweating dock workers who hustled to and fro, unloading cargo. There was lumber from the northern forests on the shores of the Great Lakes. There were big barrels of rum or molasses from New Orleans, far down at the mouth of the Mississippi; bales of cotton from other river towns; all kinds of manufactured goods from eastern cities.

Steam engines clattered and clanked as they hoisted some of the goods to the upper floors of huge warehouses, where they would be stored for a while. Other goods were loaded into wagons and hauled away at once.

Piled on the docks were still other goods, waiting to be stowed aboard the ships. Some were bound down the river, for the west and south. Some were bound north and east, by way of the Great Lakes. Ten years before, when the Illinois and Michigan Canal was finished, commerce had started to grow by leaps and bounds.

Now Chicago folk could boast, with good reason, that their city was "Queen of the Lakes."

The canal, however, was only one part of the story. Big black locomotives puffed out clouds of smoke as they chugged back and forth in the railroad yards scattered throughout the city. A small railroad, the Galena and Chicago Union, had started to run westward out of Chicago in 1848. During the years since then, more than ten other railroads had entered the city from all directions.

The trains brought cattle, grain and other crops from the fertile farmlands of Illinois, Wisconsin,

Courtesy Chicago Historical Society

This 1857 view of Chicago shows part of the
growing city. Ships of all kinds crowd the Chicago
River as boxcars are loaded in a railroad yard.

Michigan and Indiana. They brought thousands of passengers as well. Some were Irish or German or Swedish families from far across the sea, seeking new homes in America. Many were farm folk who had just come to see the sights. Others were businessmen, ready to buy or to sell.

Perhaps Sarah Lawrence was a little abashed by all the hustle and bustle as she and James made their way to their boardinghouse.

Most of the streets still lay deep in mud or dust. Many were cluttered with trash and garbage, thrown out and left there by careless people. The sidewalks were made of wooden boards. Some stood as much as ten feet higher than the

Trains like this one chugged along the banks of Lake Michigan, carrying goods and people.

streets. In other places, they were right down at street level. Thus, people had to keep climbing up and down wooden stairs as they walked along.

There were plenty of bad things about Chicago— no one could deny that. The city had some miserable slums, known by such names as Kilgubbin, Kansas, and Conley's Patch. There were hundreds of rough saloons and gambling dens. But there were lots of pleasant sights, too, other than the mud, the dirt, and the ugly, crowded streets.

Fashionable ladies went about in pretty bonnets and flaring skirts of crinoline. This was a cotton fabric, stiffened with strands of horsehair and linen. Often the bottoms of the skirts were spread out by big hoops, making them resemble huge bells. Hoop skirts were high style in those days. They must have been very awkward to get around in, but no lady of fashion would dream of not wearing one.

Dancing was popular too, that year of 1858. Another visitor described a grand ball he attended:

> Beauties of every hue flittered in the mazes of the shifting dance, and hundreds of fair ones attired in elegant costumes of every color of the rainbow mingled with somber black coats in the glare of a thousand lights.

Such grand affairs were only for wealthy people,

On frosty winter days Chicagoans whirled across the ice in the city's great covered skating rink.

of course. But plainer folk could have fun at church suppers, or go on picnics or hayrides in the open country around Chicago. In the winter there were sleigh rides, with bells tinkling merrily on the horses' harnesses. Many people liked to go ice skating, too, in the huge covered rink right in the center of the city.

The skaters glided gracefully over the ice to the tune of lively music played by a German band. When they grew tired, the ladies and gentlemen could sit down and have a cup of coffee, while the boys and girls drank delicious hot chocolate.

50

Truly, Chicago offered something for nearly everyone. We don't know how James and Sarah Lawrence got along in their new home. Maybe they did save enough money to buy the farm they dreamed of. At any rate, like thousands of other people, they probably found their proper place in the teeming, busy city.

Like thousands of others, also, they probably never thought very much about the great events that were brewing. Soon those events would test the mettle, not only of Chicago, but of the whole nation.

Stirring times were on the way.

7. The Wigwam

Horns tooted and drums went rat-a-tat-tat. Down the street came a brass band, blaring out a lively tune. Behind the band marched yelling men, carrying big signs on poles.

WILLIAM H. SEWARD FOR PRESIDENT, said the signs.

Crowds of people on the plank sidewalks pushed and jostled one another. Some of the men looked very dignified in their long coats of dark broadcloth and tall hats shaped like stovepipes. Others were more roughly dressed. Their trouser legs were stuffed into the tops of their heavy boots. Many were chewing tobacco. They talked and argued in loud voices.

Fine ladies in crinolines and hoop skirts craned their necks to see. So did poorer women in plainer dresses, with shawls around their shoulders. Boys and girls pushed and squirmed, trying to peer around the grown-ups. Some of the men cheered as the parade marched past. But some jeered, too.

Then more bands marched down the street, and more men carried signs on poles. Most of these signs also bore William H. Seward's name. A few read: HONEST ABE, THE RAIL SPLITTER. Again some folk cheered, while some hooted in derision. Many of the men grew angry. They shouted, and shook their fists at each other.

All the marchers headed toward a huge building on Lake Street, just south of the Chicago River. It was the same spot where the old Sauganash Tavern had once stood. But the tavern had been torn down to make room for this big, new hall. It was called the Wigwam, and it was far from attractive. In fact, it looked much like an immense box made of pine lumber. On this day, however, history was going to be made there.

It was Friday, May 18, 1860. The Republican party was about to choose its candidate to run for president of the United States in November.

Never before had a great national party met in Chicago, so it was a great honor for the city. In addition, the November election was sure to be one of the most important ever held.

For many long years, the nation had been split by a serious disagreement. People who lived in the southern states believed that it was proper for them to keep black people as slaves. Northern people thought that slavery was wrong. As time passed, feelings on both sides had become more and more bitter. Now some southern states were threatening to leave the Union and set up a new nation of their own.

If that happened, there might be war between North and South. A great deal would depend on the next man to be elected president.

No Republican ever had held that office. This year, though, everybody knew that the Democrats were fighting fiercely among themselves over the

The Wigwam—site of the Republican convention

slavery question. Therefore, the man whom the Republicans selected here in Chicago would be very likely to win in November.

Who would he be?

Many people thought William H. Seward had the best chance. He was a good man, and a famous United States senator from New York. Many important leaders were backing him. They had a strong organization and a lot of money to spend.

Abraham Lincoln, the other leading candidate, was a lawyer from Springfield, Illinois. His parents had been poor. Lincoln himself had been born in a crude log cabin. As a young man, he had had to work hard at such jobs as splitting rails to make fences. He was not as well known as Seward, and his backers were plain, small-town fellows without much money.

They were shrewd and determined, though. They meant to win the nomination for Abe Lincoln, no mistake about it.

Dozens of American flags hung inside the Wigwam. The walls and the speaker's platform were decorated with red, white, and blue draperies. The place was jammed with people. They filled every seat and stood packed in the aisles. Many who wanted to root for Seward couldn't get in, because the Lincoln people had got there first. They shoved and struggled, to no avail. Fist-fights broke out, making the ladies scream in fright.

Illinois' own Abe Lincoln received the presidential nomination at the 1860 Republican convention.

In the end, huge crowds had to wait in the streets outside, milling about impatiently.

Inside the Wigwam the meeting came to order. A man stood up and made a speech, nominating Seward. His people clapped and shouted. Then Abraham Lincoln was nominated. This time the noise was like a mighty clap of thunder.

Disgusted Seward men called that noise "the Lincoln yawp." One of them said later: "It was worse than a shout. It was an unbridled shriek such as I never heard before or since. It made the Wigwam quiver. It made a cold sweat come out on the brows of the New York delegation...."

Finally the noise died down. A few other men were nominated. But everyone knew the contest was between William Seward and Abe Lincoln. The voting began, men from each state voting in turn. When they finished, Seward had 173½ votes. Lincoln was second, with 102. But a man needed 233 votes in order to be nominated.

Again each state cast its votes. Seward still led with 182½. But Lincoln had gained too. He had 181.

The third time around, Lincoln took the lead with 231½ votes. Then four men from Ohio jumped up. They had already voted for another candidate, but now they changed their minds. They too cast their votes for Abe Lincoln. That did it. Lincoln men whooped and yelled as other states swung over to their side.

The voting ended. A breathless hush fell when the chairman of the convention rose to announce the result:

"Abraham Lincoln, of Illinois, is selected as your candidate for president of the United States."

Once more the "Lincoln yawp" rang out, louder than before. Men and women hugged each other. They danced in the aisles, shouting with joy. One Lincoln backer was so excited he smashed his new silk hat over a Seward man's head.

Other Lincoln men had hoisted a cannon to the roof of the Wigwam. They fired it: BA-ROOM! Steamboats in the river blew their whistles. So did locomotives in every railroad yard. Church bells rang. A mighty shout went up from the

crowds outside the Wigwam. Hats, handkerchiefs, and umbrellas were tossed high into the air.

Chicago folk went wild with delight. Abe Lincoln was the one they had wanted all along. He was a man after Chicago's own heart: plain, homely, strong, and honest. They felt sure he would win.

When November came, Abe Lincoln did win. Though few people could foresee it, he would become one of our nation's greatest presidents.

Still, however, the dispute over slavery was not settled. Soon, one by one, southern states declared that they were no longer a part of the United States. There was only one way to save the Union then.

Civil war broke out between North and South.

8. Chicago At War

"Left! Right! Left!" the drill sergeants shouted. "Hup, hup, hup—!"

Up and down the broad field that ran along the lakefront of Chicago, squads of soldiers marched back and forth. They wore baggy red trousers, red caps tilted at jaunty angles, and short jackets shining with bright gold braid. They were patriotic young fellows who had joined special regiments raised by some of the city's leading men.

Their gaudy uniforms were patterned after those worn by French soldiers called Zouaves, in far-off Africa. The Zouaves were famous for the brave and fierce way they fought. Now these young Americans called themselves Zouaves too, because they were eager to fight bravely and fiercely for the Union.

Chicago was going to war.

Through the streets marched other soldiers, clad in plainer uniforms of blue. Still others crowded every railroad station. The city's central location made it the best place for soldiers from all the surrounding states to gather. Long trains full of soldiers pulled out nearly every day, bound for the battlefields in the south and east.

Those battlefields were far away from Chicago. But even the people who stayed at home had a big, important part to play in the war.

The Union armies needed supplies of every description. They needed guns, ammunition, wagons, uniforms, shoes, and, above all, food. Never, even during the best of times in the past, had business boomed as it did during these war years.

A man named Cyrus McCormick had come to Chicago in 1847 and started to manufacture a machine which he had invented to cut and harvest grain. Farmers using such a machine could harvest their crops with far fewer workers than when the job was done by hand. Now, with so many farm boys away at war, McCormick reapers were badly needed on the vast wheat farms of the northwest. Workmen in his factory on the north side of the river kept busy night and day, turning them out.

Cattle were kept in Chicago's stockyards until they were slaughtered in meat-packing plants.

Soon Chicago's storehouses were bulging with grain hauled in by the railroads. Trainloads of cattle and hogs came rolling in—more of them than ever before. The meat-packing plants along the Chicago River could no longer handle so many. Some businessmen got together and decided they should build a great new stockyard.

Crews of men went to work on a large tract of land at the southwest edge of the city. They built railroad sidings for the cattle cars. New stock pens and packing plants began to rise like magic. Streets were laid out, and sewers dug. Some folk complained that the cows and pigs were going to have a nicer city than the people

63

themselves. But in years to come, a poet named Carl Sandburg would call Chicago "hog butcher to the world"—and it would be true.

All this activity brought lots of money to the city. Everybody had a good job, and wages were high. There was a bad side to it as well, however.

With so many new people flocking into Chicago, parts of the city became filthier and more crowded than ever. Many of the newcomers were criminals, looking for easy money. At night, in the glare of sputtering gaslights, the streets were jammed with soldiers home on leave and with workmen eager to spend their wages on gambling and drinking. They were often cheated or robbed, or even murdered.

One street in the middle of Chicago came to be known as "Hair-trigger Block," because so many men were shot there.

Whenever news came of a battle fought in some far-off place, great crowds of people gathered in front of every newspaper office. They waited patiently for lists to be put up, giving the names of soldiers who had been killed or wounded. Afterward, many of the women went away, sobbing softly for sons or husbands or sweethearts they would never see again.

Others, perhaps, whispered little prayers of thanksgiving. But they too were sober-faced and worried, for they knew there were other battles yet to come.

For four long, bitter years such scenes as this went on. Then, one April day in 1865, came the news everyone had waited for. The Southern army had surrendered; the war was over. But soon there came bad news, too. President Abraham Lincoln had been murdered, by a man filled with spite and hatred because the South had lost.

The dead president was brought home to Illinois in a special train. The locomotive and all the cars were draped in black cloth, to show the nation's grief. Throngs of people stood beside the railroad track as the train chugged slowly into Chicago.

They took their hats off and bowed their heads in sadness and respect. Church bells tolled solemnly, and cannons fired a salute.

Other crowds filed slowly through Chicago's courthouse, where Abe Lincoln lay in state. For three days the city mourned. A thousand men with flaming torches marched to the railroad yard on the night the funeral train pulled out again, taking Lincoln home to Springfield. Many of them were not ashamed to be seen weeping.

Then, like the rest of the nation—sadly, but thankfully—Chicago turned to the days of peace.

9. October 1871

In a large Chicago auditorium on Saturday night, October 7, 1871, a tall man with a pointed beard and a long, sharp nose stood up to give a lecture.

No doubt the audience listened to him with great interest, for he was Mr. George Francis Train, a famous author and world traveler. What he said has long since been forgotten, though, except for just one thing. During his speech, Train suddenly raised his hand and cried out:

"This is the last public address that will be delivered within these walls. A terrible calamity is impending over the city of Chicago. More I cannot say; more I dare not utter...."

He left the city that same night, without explaining what he had meant. But nobody seemed very frightened about it. Next day a newspaper editor wrote scornfully that Mr. Train was "the prince of blatherskites"—and most Chicago folk probably agreed. They were proud of their city, and they didn't want to hear any gloomy talk about it.

We can't blame them for that. As the years passed swiftly, following the end of the Civil War, Chicago had grown to be one of the greatest cities in the United States.

More than 300,000 people lived there. The city stretched for six miles from north to south along the Lake Michigan shore. It was three miles from the lake to the western city limits. The many railroads running in and out of Chicago made it the biggest transportation center in the world. The huge Union Stockyards, begun during the war, were also the biggest in the world. Ships from every port on the Great Lakes still crowded the Chicago River, loading and unloading cargo.

The river, which forked about a half mile west of Lake Michigan, divided the city into three parts.

In the South Section, between the south fork and the lake, lay the main business district, with stores and office buildings. Between the lake and the north fork of the river was the North Section. It was spacious and beautiful, for many of

Chicago's wealthiest people had built fine, large homes there. West of the forks was an area of busy factories, along with the small, plain houses of the people who worked in them.

What "terrible calamity" could befall such a big and bustling city?

The years of growth had brought many changes for the better. One was a new water system. People no longer had to use the foul, stinking water from the Chicago River for drinking and bathing.

A tunnel had been dug for two miles out under the bottom of Lake Michigan. Pure, fresh lake

In 1866 carriages and horse-drawn streetcars shared this crudely cobbled street in the business district.

water flowed through it, into the city. There it was pumped to the top of a tall stone tower. When it flowed down out of the tower, it had enough pressure to carry it through pipes to all parts of Chicago.

A newspaper reporter wrote, somewhat jokingly, about the improvement:

> The cleansing properties of the new water are wonderful. Children whose faces have been washed in it have been lost and never found. Their mothers cannot recognize them. In time, it is expected that many young children, whom nobody knows, will be recognized by their parents.

Cars drawn by horses now ran over rails laid in some of Chicago's main streets. Those streets were paved, often with wooden blocks used in place of bricks or cobblestones. Most others, however, were not yet paved. In dry weather they still were rutted and dusty. When it rained, they became mires of sticky mud, as in years past.

Still, the city was doing its best to improve itself.

Many of the lowest, swampiest areas had been filled in. Some large buildings had been lifted bodily. The earth beneath them was dug out, and thousands of powerful jacks placed there. Then, at a foreman's signal, thousands of workmen slowly

Courtesy Chicago Historical Society

The buildings and sidewalks of this entire block were raised far above the roadway while swampy land was filled in and new foundations built.

began to turn the jacks. In this way, a building could be raised literally "by its bootstraps," as the saying went.

Despite such marvellous feats of engineering, though, Chicago was very largely a wooden city. Many miles of sidewalks still were built of flimsy planks. Most of the twenty-seven bridges that spanned the Chicago River were of wood. So was nearly every house.

There were many buildings of brick or stone, of course. But lumber was so cheap that most builders preferred to use it. Sometimes the wood

72

was carved and painted to look like stone. The fronts of many of the bigger, newer buildings were decorated with plates or tall pillars of cast iron. Wooden church steeples were often covered with thin sheets of tin or copper.

Nevertheless, fire was a constant danger in Chicago. Perhaps George Francis Train knew that when he made his strange prediction.

The people themselves knew it, for the city had had some bad fires in the past. But they seldom worried about it. The city had a very fine fire department with no fewer than seventeen big steam fire engines. There were no telephones in those days, but fires were reported to central headquarters by telegraph as soon as they broke out. In addition, a watchman was always on duty, looking out over the city from a tower on top of the courthouse.

In the 1870's few cities had any better protection.

A steam fire engine of those days had a tall, upright boiler with a furnace or firebox underneath, and a big water pump mounted in front. Both pump and boiler were of brass, or a metal called nickel-plate, and the firemen kept them polished till they glittered. Teams of spirited horses were always ready, so they could be hitched up at a moment's notice.

Galloping madly to answer an alarm, one of these engines made a grand sight. The bright red

wheels bounced and clattered over the rough street. Clouds of smoke poured out of the boiler. Foam flew from the horses' mouths. Shouting men and boys ran along behind, anxious to help fight the fire.

It was no wonder Chicago folk took pride in such machines, and gave them fancy names like the *Waubansia,* the *Winnebago,* the *Long John,* the *Little Giant,* and so on. They could handle any fire that broke out, the people thought.

The danger was much worse than usual, though, this October of 1871. All summer long, scarcely any rain had fallen. Trees, shrubbery—and houses, too—were so dry they could blaze up in an instant. Hot winds blew in from the prairie around Chicago, making everything drier still.

Mr. Train may have been thinking of that, too, when he spoke on Saturday night.

10. Mrs. O'Leary's Cow

De Koven Street was a dusty, dingy little street in the West Section of Chicago, some way south of the crowded factory district. The O'Leary family lived there in a small wooden house at number 137.

There was nothing very remarkable about Patrick O'Leary or his plump, pleasant wife Catherine. They were plain, hardworking folk like hundreds of others who lived around them. Catherine kept five cows in a barn behind their house. In order to make a little extra money, she ran a milk route in the neighborhood. That wasn't unusual. Many Chicago families kept cows, or other livestock, in those days.

We remember the O'Learys only because a fire broke out in their barn on Sunday evening, October 8.

A neighbor named Daniel Sullivan was sitting against a fence across the street, enjoying the nice warm evening. He saw the flames through a barn window and jumped up with a yell:

"Fire! Fire!"

Hobbling, because he had a wooden leg, Sullivan hurried to the barn. Frantically he started to let the cows out of their stalls. But the hot fire quickly drove him back outside.

Aroused by his shouting, the O'Learys tumbled out of bed. Little Mary O'Leary, only four years old, snatched her baby brother from his crib and ran into the yard. Her older brothers and sisters followed, and Patrick and Catherine too. Flames from the barn already were licking hungrily at their house.

They began to throw buckets of water over it; other neighbors ran to send in an alarm. Soon a hose cart called the *America* galloped up. Then the steam fire engine *Little Giant* arrived. Unhitching their horses—for the fire made them so nervous they were hard to manage—the firemen connected up their hoses and went to work. Streams of water splashed over the O'Learys' house.

It was saved—but now the fire was spreading farther along the block. A strong, gusty wind

A wall of flame raged through Chicago on its path of destruction, as shown by Currier and Ives.

blew from the southwest. It whirled sparks and bits of burning wood through the air, dropping them on the roofs of other houses and barns. They began to blaze up too.

From his tower atop the courthouse, a watchman saw a fiery glare in the sky. He called to the telegraph operator in a room below. In a few minutes, the alarm went out to every fire station in the city. The big courthouse bell began to ring.

All over Chicago, gongs clanged and firemen awoke. Throwing their clothes on, hitching up the horses, they leaped aboard their fire engines and clattered off. Unluckily, though, someone had made a mistake. The first alarms sent many of the engines to the wrong neighborhoods, so they were slow in getting to the fire.

They found it spreading faster and faster. Crackling and roaring, driven by the wind, a wall of flame swept steadily north and east, toward the very heart of the city.

The firemen fought bravely. Smoke blinded and choked them. The heat blistered their hands and faces, and shriveled their leather firemen's hats. Tearing the doors from burning buildings, they crouched behind them, using them as shields while they played their hoses on the flames. But the wooden doors themselves caught fire. Hoses burst in the fierce heat.

Again and again the men had to hitch up the horses and pull their engines back to safer spots. Then, with new hoses, they turned and went on fighting, but it was a losing battle. Thomas Byrne was one of many firemen who never forgot that night.

"You couldn't see anything over you but fire," he recalled later. "No clouds, no stars, nothing else but fire."

One engine, the *John Gund*, wasn't moved quickly enough. A burning building toppled down on it, and it was buried under tons of bricks. Some men remembered how the fire gleamed in

vivid colors: red and yellow, pink, gold, and various shades of blue and purple and green. The wind blew harder, whipped to a gale force by the heat. Before long, flames jumped over the river into the South Section, then into the North Section as well.

Everywhere, crowds of people were fleeing in blind fear. Wagons and carriages thundered through the streets. Frightened men hailed every hack driver, offering big sums of money if only they could be taken to some safe place. Many folk, in their panic, just ran with whatever they could carry from their homes.

A little barefooted girl was seen with four tiny puppies in a box. A man ran by with a rooster sitting on his shoulder. Others carried bits of food, furniture—all sorts of things. The owner of a jewelry store stood in his doorway, handing watches and rings to passersby. No doubt he thought that was better than letting them burn.

Some men brought kegs of gunpowder and touched them off, blowing up buildings in the fire's path. They thought that might stop it, but they were wrong. The flames roared on.

Tugboats churned up and down the river, towing away the ships that were moored there. When they blew their whistles, calling for the drawbridges to open and let them pass, the confusion in the crowded streets became worse than ever. Soon many of the bridges were burning also.

Chicago people were proud of their big new pumping station in the North Section, which supplied water to the whole city. It was supposed to be fireproof, for it was built of stone. The wind smashed a blazing timber through the roof, however, starting a fire inside. The roof was made of slate but the beams that supported it were made of wood. They burned away, the roof fell in with a crash, and the pumps stopped.

Presently, weary firemen saw the streams of water from their hoses dwindle away to nothing. The water mains were empty. After that the fire engines were useless, except for a few that were able to pump water directly from Lake Michigan or the Chicago River.

By that time, it scarcely mattered. Michael Conway, one of the firemen, said later that he didn't think the fire could possibly have been stopped "unless you picked it up and threw it into the lake."

As the long night passed, thousands of homeless people gathered on a barren stretch by the lakeshore, known as the Sands. Some had pitiful little bundles of household goods beside them. Some were wealthy men and women wearing costly clothing and jewelry. Lost dogs and cats, cows and horses wandered among them. One little girl wept bitterly because she had lost her pet canary.

The people crouched there, miserable and forlorn. On one side of them, the fire still raged.

Thousands of terrified citizens gathered on the lakeshore as the fire devoured their city.

On the other was the lake, churned into stormy waves by the wind. Suddenly, smoke from a burning lumberyard nearby rolled over the Sands in a choking cloud. Sparks and red-hot cinders rained down.

There was a wild rush for the lake. Many people stood knee-deep in the waves, splashing water over themselves so their clothing wouldn't catch fire. Several brave men buried their wives and children in the sand, leaving tiny holes through which they could breathe. The men watched all night long, pouring water on the sand to cool it in the scorching heat.

Thus the dismal hours passed till Monday's dawn.

The fire burned on. Finally the wind shifted, blowing against the flames. Still they burned, though not so rapidly now. Then, late Monday night, rain began to fall. Slowly the fire flickered and died at last.

The Great Chicago Fire was over. No one ever knew how it had started. Probably no one ever will.

Over the years, a story grew that Mrs. O'Leary had gone out to milk one of her cows that fateful Sunday evening. The cow kicked her lantern over; some dry straw blazed up—and so it began. But that isn't a very likely story. Catherine O'Leary always denied it. No doubt she was telling the truth, for we know her whole family was in bed when Daniel Sullivan first saw the burning barn.

To this day, though, the legend is still told of the famous cow that burned Chicago down.

11. Out of the Ashes

"When we lay down, away from the crowd, and I knew I had my husband and children safe, I felt so rich—I have never in my life felt so rich!"

Mrs. Charles Forsberg, the woman who wrote that, was just one of the thousands who had lost everything they owned in the fire. Yet she was more fortunate than some others. Perhaps as many as 300 people had been killed. No one knew for sure, because many bodies never were found. Hundreds more suffered burns, or other injuries.

Three and a half square miles of Chicago lay in ashes. The whole business district had been wiped out, along with most of the largest, finest homes. More than $200 million worth of property was destroyed.

Some days later, an article in the *Chicago Tribune* gave a vivid description of the city:

What had hours before been the mart of commerce was now an indescribable chaos of broken columns, fallen walls, streets covered with debris, melted metal, charred and blackened trees standing like spectres....The tall spires of churches, the Courthouse dome, the stately blocks...the noted landmarks ...everything had disappeared.

Once again, however, as they had so many

times before, the people of Chicago showed their spunk. Some, it was true, were so badly discouraged that they left the city forever. But most were like Margaret O'Toole, an old woman who had always sold hot roasted chestnuts at a little stand on Lake Street, in the business district.

On Tuesday morning after the fire, she was at her stand as usual. It was said that she was the first Chicago merchant to reopen for business.

A real estate man named William Kerfoot hurriedly knocked together a rude little shack among

After the fire—Chicago in ruins

the ruins. That was his new office. Over the door he hung a sign:

All Gone but Wife, Children, and ENERGY!

Nothing could beat that kind of spirit. And the bigger businessmen of the city—men who had lost millions of dollars—were just as quick to show they were not beaten.

Marshall Field and Levi Leiter, for example, were partners in a big department store. Now it was gone, with its whole stock of goods. But Field and Leiter had signs put up at once, telling everyone who worked for them that they would be paid the wages they had coming. New goods were ordered, on credit. Within three weeks the store was doing business again, in an old horse barn near the burned-out area.

Every newspaper office in the city was destroyed; but Joseph Medill, owner of the *Tribune*, managed to rent a small printshop in the West Section. Its one old press had to be operated by hand, and there was only a scanty supply of type. Nevertheless, copies of the *Tribune* were being run off by the Wednesday after the fire. Another newspaper, the *Journal*, printed its first edition on sheets of paper less than six inches square.

All over Chicago, men and women turned to the big job of starting their lives anew. People everywhere were glad to help. Carloads of food

Faith in their city and boundless energy helped
the people of Chicago to rebuild quickly.

Citizens left homeless by the fire camp out in crude shelters on the shore of Lake Michigan.

and clothing were sent from other cities. In many places money was collected for Chicago's needy folk. Soup kitchens were opened, providing free meals to all who were hungry. Homeless families were taken in by the lucky ones whose houses had not burned.

A popular songwriter hastily dashed off a poem about the disaster. Here is one of its verses:

Ruins! Ruins! Far and wide
From the river and lake to the prairie side.
   Dreary, dreary, the darkness falls
While the autumn winds moan through
      blackened walls.
But see! The bright rift in the cloud

And hear the great voice from the shore!
  Our city shall rise!
  Yes, she shall rise!
Queen of the west once more!

Maybe that wasn't very good poetry, but it showed how the people felt. And their city *did* rise again, through faith and hard work.

Today, of course, Chicago is one of the world's great cities. It still is a bustling railroad and manufacturing center. Giant jet planes fly in and out of its busy airport. Where wooden buildings once straggled along muddy streets, tall skyscrapers of steel and concrete and glass now reach toward the stars.

If Louis Jolliet could come back nowadays—or the black fur trader, Point du Sable—or the Potawatomis whose war dance frightened the town so badly—they would never recognize the marshy old crossing place they knew.

Glossary

blatherskites: people who speak foolishly

breechclouts: strips of hide or cloth worn around the hips by some Indian men in warm weather. They are also called loincloths or breechcloths.

broadcloth: cotton, silk, or wool cloth that has a smooth texture

buckskin: soft leather made from deer or elk skins

calamity: a disaster resulting in great sorrow or terrible loss

commerce: large-scale buying and selling of goods between cities, states, or countries

gaudy: overly decorated with loud colors in poor taste

grog: a drink consisting of rum or whiskey mixed with water

jaunty: unconcerned, carefree, and cheerful

massacre: violent murdering of a large number of people

masts: tall, upright poles on ships or boats, used to support sails

militiamen: citizens who receive military training so they can help in an emergency, even though they are not regular soldiers

mires: soft, wet, muddy areas of ground

musket: a long-barreled firearm used before the invention of the rifle

portage: a crossing place where boats or goods are transported on land from one body of water to another

rogue: a mischievous, worthless fellow

schooner: a large sailing ship with two or more masts and sails

slate: hard rock, blue-gray in color, which splits easily into thin, smooth layers

stockyard: a place where cattle, sheep, pigs, etc., are kept in pens until they are slaughtered and sent to market

sultry: extremely hot and damp, without a breeze

tanneries: places where leather is made from animal hide

Index